# Cousin Beatie

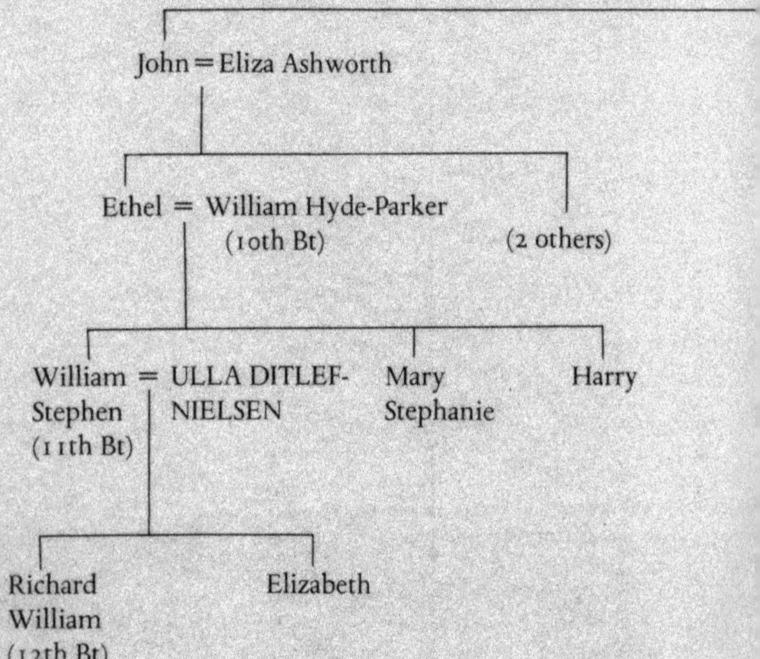
John = Eliza Ashworth
Ethel = William Hyde-Parker
(10th Bt)
(2 others)
William Stephen (11th Bt)
ULLA DITLEF-NIELSEN
Mary Stephanie
Harry
Richard William (12th Bt)
Elizabeth

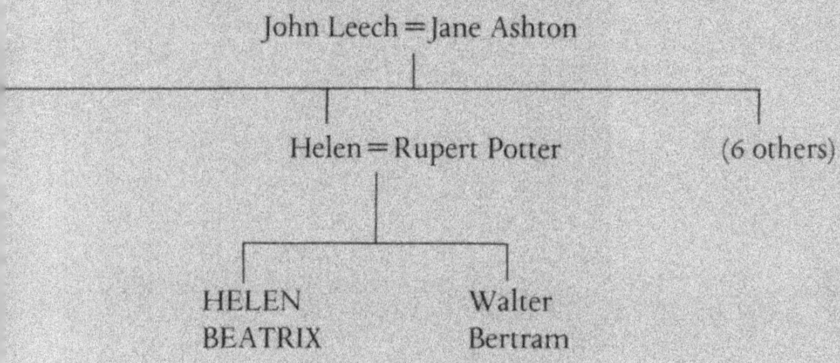


A Family Tree
showing the relationship
between
Beatrix Potter
and
Ulla Hyde Parker

# PUBLISHER'S NOTE

*Beatrix Potter came to know and love Melford Hall through the marriage of her cousin Ethel Leech to Sir William Hyde Parker, 10th Baronet, whose beautiful home it was. The author of this book married their son, William Stephen, who became the 11th Baronet. There is a family tree on the endpapers for readers who are interested in tracing relationships.*

*When Beatrix Potter married William Heelis (Cousin Willie in this book), she became very involved in the farming life of the Lake District, giving up, to a large extent, her writing and illustrating, but she left behind her some lovely mementos of her visits to Melford Hall in the form of delicate watercolours and sketches of her surroundings, some of which are reproduced here as further embellishment to this unique little 'cameo' of the famous author and artist.*

# Cousin Beatie

## A MEMORY OF BEATRIX POTTER

by Ulla Hyde Parker

FREDERICK WARNE

FREDERICK WARNE

UK | USA | Canada | Ireland | Australia
India | New Zealand | South Africa

Frederick Warne is part of the Penguin Random House group of companies
whose addresses can be found at global.penguinrandomhouse.com.

www.penguin.co.uk www.puffin.co.uk www.ladybird.co.uk

Penguin Random House UK

First published 1981
This edition published 2016
001



Picture credits: front cover and page 21 courtesy of Frederick Warne & Co. Ltd; back cover courtesy of NT/Fisheye images; page 45 courtesy of East Anglian Daily Times; pages 10 and 15 courtesy of the Trustees of the Linder Collection; pages 13, 30, 32, 37, 39, 42 and 43 courtesy of the Hyde Parker Family; pages 16, 26 and 29 courtesy of the Victoria and Albert Museum; page 22 courtesy of NTPL/NT Images; page 41 courtesy of private collector



Printed and bound in Great Britain by CPI Group (UK) Ltd, Croydon
A CIP catalogue record for this book is available from the British Library

ISBN: 978–0–241–29753–7

All correspondence to:
Frederick Warne, Penguin Random House Children's
80 Strand, London WC2R 0RL

*To the memory of*

*Willie*

*my dearest husband*

The corner of the gazebo in the garden at Melford Hall, a watercolour by Beatrix Potter

# Cousin Beatie

Cousin Beatie! What do I remember about her? I remember how much Willie spoke about her as soon as we had married and I was installed at Melford. He kept on saying 'You must meet Cousin Beatie. You will understand and love her and she you.' And when I asked, 'But who is Cousin Beatie?' his answer was, 'My mother's cousin, Beatrix Potter, who lives in the Lake District at Sawrey,' and he would tell me how she rebelled against her parents and their conventional life, how she started writing letters to the small son of her former companion and German teacher, and how she kept him amused by telling him about Peter Rabbit, illustrating her letters with drawings of this Peter Rabbit. He told me how this became the start of the children's stories which she later wrote and illustrated so beautifully in colour.

I became intrigued by this Cousin Beatie.

After my engagement to Willie, my mother and I went to Melford for Mother to be introduced to my future home and family. I was put into the west room, as it was then called. 'Cousin Beatie,' I was told, 'always stayed here when she came to Melford. She loved this room, and the cages with her animals were put in this little tower room.'

'Animals?' I exclaimed. 'What animals?'

Willie replied, 'Oh, when we were children we just loved it when she arrived, for she always brought a cage with mice, another with a hamster or a porcupine, and a third with something else in it. It was such fun for us children. We used to gather at the front door to see these cages of animals being brought out of the car among her other baggage. How exciting it was!'

Cousin Beatie loved animals. They were her real friends; she studied them or played with them for hours on end and they went with her wherever she went. She sketched them, making beautiful drawings or watercolours and revealing their individual beauty and character, even personality. Personality is really the right word, for her animals did become people, real people, by the time she had depicted them in line and colour, making them do and say all sorts of things. Her animals became people—people animals.

But by now Cousin Beatie was getting too old to travel about, and so it was for us to go up to the Lakes to visit her at Sawrey.

When at Melford, Cousin Beatie had not spoken a great deal to the children, though she read her stories to them to find out their reactions. Most of her time had been spent out of doors drawing and painting. She drew some of the *Jeremy Fisher* illustrations at our ancient fish ponds, and while there she sketched Melford as seen over these ponds. (This book was dedicated to Stephanie Hyde Parker.) She drew the large fireplace in the Hall, and another in what was then the servants' hall. She sketched a view of the winding staircase in one of our turrets and one of a set of Chippendale chairs which then stood in our entrance hall. She drew the four-poster beds and, finally, when she was leaving, made drawings of Old Mr. Benjamin Bunny and Jemima Puddle-Duck with the sandy-whiskered gentleman in the visitors' book.

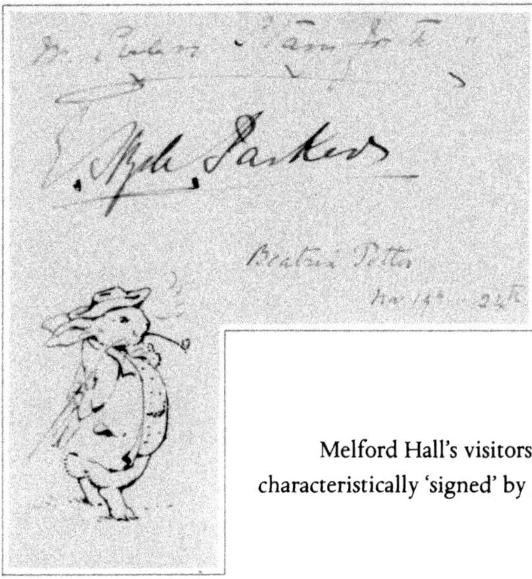


Melford Hall's visitors' books,
characteristically 'signed' by Beatrix Potter

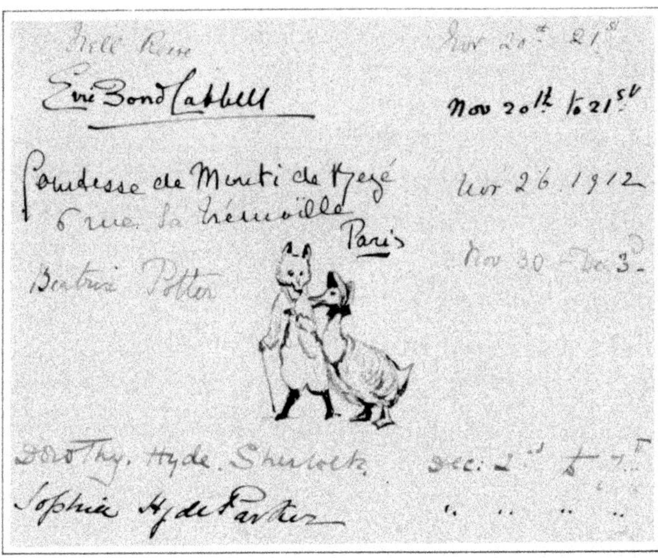

The day came when Willie and I were to visit Cousin Beatie for a few days on our way to Scotland. How well I remember my surprise at driving up to an ordinary cottage. A lane led up to it, at the end of which was an old barn on the left and the entrance to one end of a long narrow cottage on the right. The entrance opened into the kitchen, through which we went into a small darkish room furnished with some oak court cupboards, and from there into the dining-cum-living room. Cousin Beatie came to greet us—a short, round little lady with a smiling rosy face and small bright blue twinkling eyes.

I sensed great warmth but at the same time great reserve, even shyness. She wore a thick brown tweed skirt of natural colour and a heavy knitted jersey, strong leather shoes and one could just glimpse the hand-knitted woollen stocking beneath her long, somewhat full skirt. A small black straw hat was held in place by a piece of elastic under the chin, just like a child would wear. Then Cousin Willie, her husband, appeared. What a kindly face! With a fresh complexion, grey hair and a warm smile he seemed so relaxed and straightforward. He obviously was an uncomplicated person with a practical approach to life.

Back in the kitchen stood a middle-aged sturdy north country woman, busy preparing our lunch. It smelt good. The kitchen was spotless, with its pale silver-grey scrubbed kitchen table and its stone-flagged floor. (I later discovered that the beautiful sheen on the floor was achieved by washing the stone flags with milk and water.) The room beyond was a glorious muddle. An Indian shawl covered part of the large dining-room table. On this a newspaper was spread on which stood inkpot, pen and paint box,

The fireplace in the Main Hall at Melford, an unfinished watercolour by Beatrix Potter

A sketch of a Chippendale chair at Melford Hall, by Beatrix Potter

besides several sheets of paper. Next to these stood the bread-board and a dish with cheeses. I found out later that these items always remained there, for this was their permanent abode. A fine white damask cloth covered the other end of the table, where places were laid for the four of us. The chairs round the table were beautiful Chippendale chairs. On the wall to the right, between two long French windows, stood a fine mahogany bureau, its shelves filled with books and papers leaning in all directions; some books were standing, others had fallen down flat.

By the fireplace opposite the door were comfortable armchairs, which had obviously been used for years. The whole place was in need of a good dusting and turn out—at least this was what I felt. Yet its homely unselfconscious charm appealed to me. The room was certainly lived in and it showed that the lives of those who occupied it were filled with a multitude of interests, for there were books on sheep breeding and papers from sheep sales and flower seeds, spread out to dry on old sheets of paper by the French windows.

There was one thing peculiar to this room—something very noticeable—and that was a strange pungent smell. It was a smell I had never come across before and it was most unpleasant. The closer you approached to the fireplace the stronger it became. Where I was placed in the armchair to the right of the fire I noticed there was a door in the wall just by my side and that whatever the smell was, it was coming from behind this door. I wondered what it could be. What was in there?

But soon my attention was drawn back to Cousin Beatie and her husband, for I had to answer many questions about Melford, Denmark and my family.

Then we rose. The windows behind me looked out to a typical cottage garden which ran down towards a meadow. In the garden grew flowers and vegetables, mingled in great profusion; and here and there stood flower pots with seedlings, or plants which had been put outside because their flowering period was over.

I was shown up to our bedroom, with its plain four-poster bed with charming, faded old-world chintz hangings. The room was very simply furnished, but another beautiful mahogany bureau stood near the windows. This one did not contain books but a multitude of china objects of all kinds and sizes, not arranged in any kind of order. They were apparently just kept there where they were safe and out of the way. (On a later visit I washed and arranged these items as well as I could, to the great delight of Cousin Beatie.)

'The bed is not very wide,' commented Cousin Beatie, 'yet may you both sleep well in it.' And she added, rather to my surprise,'If one cannot share a bed when married one cannot share anything.'

By now the black straw hat had come off and a white muslin mob cap had taken its place. It was edged with lace, and a black velvet ribbon covered the gathering threads above its frill. A few white silky curls and wisps of hair fell on her forehead. Some years later, when we had become closer friends, I made her a couple of white muslin caps like these, and she was truly pleased.

As a person, and in her way of life, she fascinated me. In the evening she showed me some of her drawings and writings. She had heard that I myself had studied art for a few years. I especially remember her drawings, or rather paintings, of fungi and how exquisite they were. Then she told me that we would go for a drive the next morning to see more of the beauty of the Lake District, also some of her farms and flocks of sheep. The men would go out fishing.

The next morning, to my amazement, a beautiful large black spotlessly clean car drew up in the rather small gap between the barn and the kitchen door. Out came the most dignified chauffeur in an equally spotless uniform, and with his gloved hand he opened the doors for Cousin Beatie and myself. I could not get over the startling contrast between the dignity of the vehicle we were to be driven in and the house in front of which it stood; nor between the smart turnout of the chauffeur and the 'get up' of his mistress, who was looking just like an ordinary farmer's wife. Yet Cousin Beatie had a presence which commanded respect. She had the self-assurance of a person who is aware of the qualities within herself, however little the world might be aware of these, and who also knows what values she upholds and stands for. Perhaps such qualities are found only in people who have suffered for their strong individuality, in people who cannot be 'shaped', since some inner compass needles constantly seem to swing back to the point of direction they have to follow.

Religion as such meant little to Cousin Beatie. At least, she attended no church. She belonged to that generation for whom mention of such matters was just not made—it was not 'decent', in some strange way—but she would talk about the beautiful language of the Bible; so the Bible she knew well.

We drove high up into the hills. What beauty! We

visited farm houses which belonged to her, and were greeted with respect but perhaps not much warmth. Mrs Heelis, as she was always called and referred to, was very much their superior. She owned their lands, a fact never forgotten, and she was an expert on sheep farming, sheep and sheepdogs. She knew intimately every acre we passed and she also understood the upkeep of the land, the farm houses and farm buildings. This became quite clear to me from the conversation, to which I was a silent audience. Her knowledge created the respect, so the obvious distance which existed between her and her tenants and employees was not simply based on social differences.

I quickly realized that her tenants stood in some awe of her; but when we reached her various shepherds, guarding large flocks of sheep, she would jump quickly out of the car, and with these men there was immediate contact, for she and they understood one another. Cousin Beatie would point with her stick at various sheep among the huge flocks and say, 'These were the ones we bought at Kendal sale. They are doing well.' 'Yes, madam,' was the answer. She and her shepherds knew the faces of their sheep individually. This made the deepest impression on me. How was it possible? I stared at the faces of the various sheep. To me they looked exactly alike.

A few days later I did discover what was behind the mysterious concealed door next to the fireplace, for Cousin Beatie said, 'Come with me; I have something to show you.'

The armchair was pushed aside and the door was opened, revealing a dark room. The strange smell became even stronger and more offensive. We entered a low dark room which looked more like a larder than a room, despite its spaciousness, for the floor was stone and the window opposite was small and covered with wire mesh. Large sheepskins were stretched out on wooden frames which were hung suspended from the ceiling. The backs of some of these skins were still pink, with a faint network of blue and red veins visible. Others had apparently hung there much longer, for their backs looked dry and cured.

After we had inspected these skins, she led me to the left side of the room, where there was a multitude of shelves filled with jars of bottled fruits and jams. Cousin Beatie surveyed with pride and satisfaction the whole contents of this rather cold and draughty place, as she said, 'When those sheepskins are washed they will be beautiful.'

Were those sheepskins, or rather previous ones, in her mind when she wrote how Mrs Tiggy-Winkle had sheepskins among the laundry she was to wash?

Herdwick sheep from *The Fairy Caravan* by Beatrix Potter

Beatrix Potter's bedroom at Melford Hall

Cousin Beatie used to speak with great warmth about Melford. 'It is a beautiful and gracious house,' she would say. 'You will look after it well, won't you, for it is worth it.' Although she begged me to do this, her own way of life seemed to suggest that she had no love or regard for a beautiful house or gracious living.

On our return from the car trip, she had taken me into a simple little spare room where stood a narrow bed covered with a faded patchwork quilt. She went to a wooden chest-of-drawers and took out of its top drawer a most beautiful Brussels lace shawl. She unfolded it carefully and handed it to me with these words: 'This belonged to my family. I want you to have it and to wear it. It will look well at Melford.' I have worn it at Melford and I have treasured that gift. Cousin Beatie and I had become friends and she invited us to return the following year for a longer visit—which we did.

Why had Cousin Beatie and I become friends? I have often wondered; for she did not invite friendships. There were people whom she had known for years, and yet one could not say that real friendship existed between them and her. She was always kind but closed up, and what lay behind other people's exteriors did not seem to interest her. Yet she was an excellent judge of character.

Did she draw closer to me because she felt I loved Melford, and that I loved it not for the life that was then led in a pre-war English country house—a life which I certainly enjoyed—but because of the beauty and the spirit of the house? For its ancient atmosphere, which spoke of generations following generations, gripped me, and so did the mature, unplanned garden and the beauty of the land and woods which surrounded it. I shared this love fully with Willie. Cousin Beatie and I often spoke about Melford. I had told her that my favourite seat was in the recess of the long yew hedge which divided the ancient fishponds from the mill stream, and how I used to love looking across the pond to see Melford mirrored in its still, clear surface. I later found that Cousin Beatie had painted a watercolour from exactly that place.

Then, of course, I was Willie's wife—Willie whom she had known since he was a small boy. There must have been love and understanding between them for it was a visit to Cousin Beatie that was among his first suggestions when he wanted to take me to meet members of the large circle of the Hyde Parker family and relations. Willie and Cousin Beatie could talk for hours about land, farming and sheep.

And what drew me towards Cousin Beatie? Her great reserve, I am sure. I longed to find out what lay behind this. In Denmark we have a saying: 'An empty house is left open. One with riches has its doors locked.' I felt that this applied to her, for watching her I would see a sensitivity and softness in her quickly moving eyes, as well as in the hardly noticeable changes of expression which moved across her face like faint ripples moving across the still waters of a tarn when touched by a breath of wind. So if one studied her, one found she was not stern, but she was 'hidden'. This made me long to open, or at least peep through a door and find her. And indeed I was granted glimpses of her hidden self.

I spent the succeeding days following her about. Again we looked at her drawings and paintings and she gave me a sketch of poppy petals arranged next to each other to form a border. 'I really did this as a design for needlework, for a coloured border for a cloth,' she said, 'but I never got down to making it.' Talking about needlework, she mentioned the beauty of smocking, and once more she led me upstairs to the little spare room with the wooden chest-of-drawers and she took out of a lower drawer two little smocks, real country smocks, which she presented to me. Their exquisite needlework was a delight to the eye. I did wonder why Cousin Beatie had among her treasures these two unused small children's smocks. For whom had they been intended?

It was a summer morning when Cousin Beatie said to me, 'Come, I have something to show you, something very precious to me.' We walked out of the house and into the meadow. I remember still the heavy dew on the young grass, for my shoes became quite wet as I walked through it. We reached the gate of Hill Top farm and proceeded up the path. I had mentioned to her the previous evening the necessity I had always felt since a child to spend a period of each day alone, in my own company, so as to 'digest' the impressions I had received and to become aware of what I myself really thought and felt. We reached the front door, and as she placed the key in its lock she said, 'It is in here I go to be quiet and still with myself.' I looked into the old front-room-cum-kitchen, completely furnished, every tiny item in its place. 'This is me,' or words to that effect, she added, 'the deepest me, the part one has to be alone with. So, you see, when Cousin Willie asked me to marry him I said yes, but I also said we cannot live here at Hill Top. We will live at Castle Cottage, as I must leave everything here as it is. So

Beatrix Potter's watercolour of Melford Hall's ancient fishpond

after I married I just locked the door and left.' And this she had certainly done, for wherever we went in that delightful little old-world cottage it looked just as if someone still lived there, except that the dust lay like a fine grey veil over everything and the delicate cobwebs spread their intricate designs in various corners.

We finally sat down silently in the little front parlour. I looked round at the faded floral carpet, the little upholstered chairs covered in faded flowered chintz, and like Cousin Beatie I fell into deep thought, for all that I had felt about Cousin Beatie and Cousin Willie was confirmed. They were certainly a happy or, perhaps better, a contented couple. They lived harmoniously alongside each other. They shared each other's interest in sheep and farming and the love of the beautiful Lake District. I remember thinking that they were like two horses in front of the same plough, they walked so steadily beside each other, leaving their furrow behind them.

But inside Cousin Beatie there was a hidden world of her own. I had seen a glimpse of this world in the delicate and so beautiful drawings she had shown me, but I also knew that what can actually be expressed is only a fraction of what has been felt. I think that it was in that silence in those still moments together in the little parlour at Hill Top that Cousin Beatie and I really drew close to one another. I understood, and she knew I did so. I remember her saying, 'You are Danish by birth; you share your nationality with Hans Christian Andersen. I tell you, Ulla, my children's stories will one day be as famous and as much read as his.' This remark startled me. I must admit I thought it presumptious at the time, but later I realized that it was not.

## *The Solitary Mouse*

(Introduction which may be skipped)

(Copyright reserved)

*I have been listening to a Danish girl distilling melody from an old spinet. Her fingers caress the yellow ivory keys. Notes come tinkling forth like the sound of a harp; like a hesitating breeze—away—far away amongst hemlocks. The limpid undertones are the song of a brook that ripples over pebbles. J. Sebastian Bach composed his minuet for such an instrument; an old-fashioned piano propped against the wainscote on seven fluted legs. The maker's name, 'Clementi', is painted above the keyboard in a wreath of tiny flowers.*

*Music strikes chords of memory. Big, golden-haired Ulla spoke of Copenhagen; of Hans Christian Andersen; of the little bronze mermaid sitting on her stone upon the strand where Danish children bathe and play beside the summer sea. She spoke of long frosts in Denmark; of skating on lakes and canals. No letter ... another month and still no letters from Denmark ... poor Denmark; poor Europe; silent behind a blank curtain of fear.*

*For me, the pretty jingling tunes bring memories of Merry Nights and of our English folk dance revival twenty years ago—the stone floored farm kitchen where first we danced 'The Boatman' and heard the swinging lilt of 'Black nag'; the loft with two fiddles where country dancers paced the 'Triumph', three in arm under arched hands. The long drive home in frosty starlight from Broughton-in-Furness with a load of rosy sleeping village girls ...*

Part of the text of one version of 'The Solitary Mouse', which was intended for a sequel to *The Fairy Caravan*, which was never completed

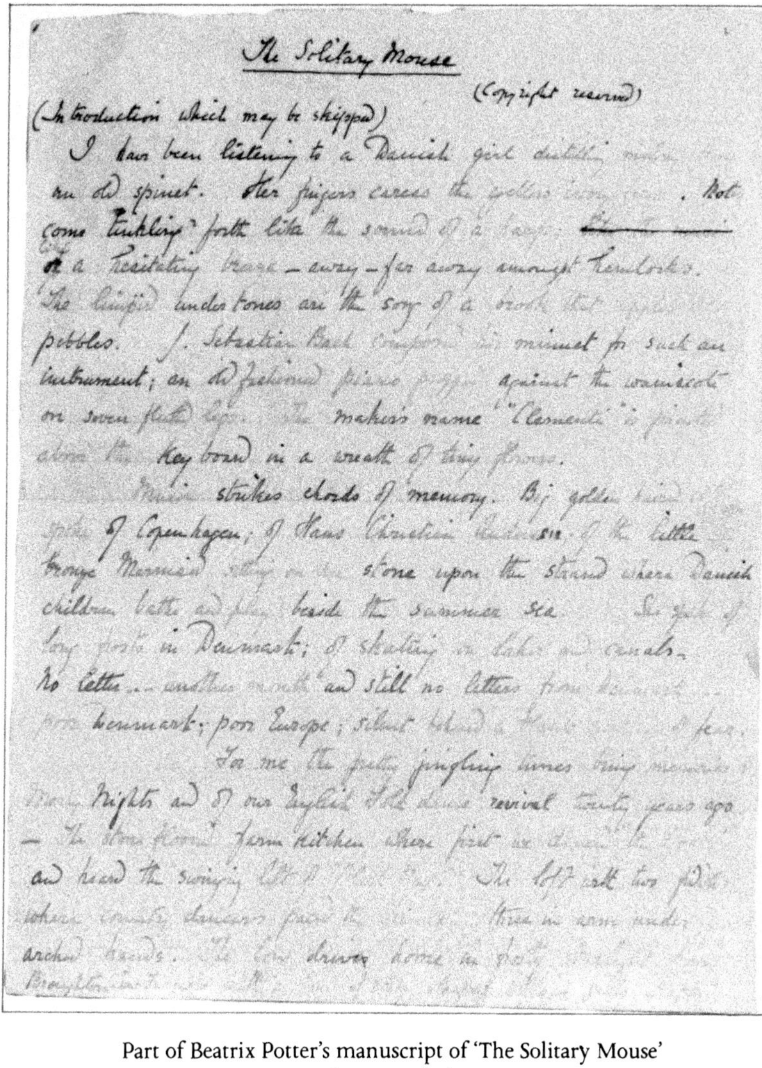
The Solitary Mouse

(Copyright reserved)

(Introduction which may be skipped)

I have been listening to a Danish girl distilling melody from an old spinet. Her fingers caress the yellow ivory keys. Notes come tinkling forth like the sound of a harp ~~[illegible]~~ or a hesitating breeze – away – far away amongst hemlocks. The limpid undertones are the song of a brook that ripples over pebbles. J. Sebastian Bach composed his minuet for such an instrument; an old fashioned piano propped against the wainscot on seven fluted legs. The maker's name "Clementi" is painted above the key board in a wreath of tiny flowers.

Music strikes chords of memory. Big golden [illegible] speaks of Copenhagen; of Hans Christian Andersen of the little bronze Mermaid sitting on the stone upon the strand where Danish children bathe and play beside the summer sea. She speaks of long frosts in Denmark; of skating on lakes and canals. No letter ... another month and still no letters from Denmark ... poor Denmark; poor Europe; silent behind a [illegible] of fear.

For me the pretty jingling tunes bring memories of [illegible] Nights and of our English Folk dance revival twenty years ago – the stone floored farm kitchen where first we danced [illegible] and heard the swinging lilt of [illegible]. The loft with two fiddles where country dancers paced [illegible] three in arm under arched hands. The [illegible] driving home in [illegible]

Part of Beatrix Potter's manuscript of 'The Solitary Mouse' (see opposite)

Signed copies of some of Beatrix Potter's books

Cousin Beatie was aware of the great talent that she had been given, and from the loneliness she had felt, from the disappointments and hurts life had inflicted on her, she had understood how to draw out the light which lies at the centre of each dark experience, however distressing, and also how to retain her true self. She had retreated into a simple life close to nature, and in that life she had seen, and drawn for others to see, the pure loveliness of a rabbit, a frog, a hedgehog, mice and other small animals; she gave them a personality and made them live. A hole in the wall with mice, the surface of a lake or pond with reeds and the broad leaves of water-lilies became miniature worlds—of far greater importance to her than even Melford Hall and its contents, for these she painted while staying at Melford. Jeremy Fisher overshadowed the old Hyde Parker admirals, even if it was Romney who painted them. Cousin Beatie gave her love where it could not be rejected, and what was important to her was Nature herself with her creatures.

That day in 1933 she gave me a copy of the first edition of *The Tailor of Gloucester* and wrote on the fly leaf *For Ulla Hyde Parker with love from Beatrix Potter. Aug. 26th 1933.*

During the following years we always visited Cousin Beatie and Cousin Willie on our way to Scotland. Cousin Beatie and I corresponded—or rather kept in touch. She wrote me such dear letters after my children were born. She was delighted that there were once more children here at Melford. Sadly her letters were burnt with much else in 1942 when a fire broke out while the army was occupying the house.

Sir William Hyde Parker at Hill Top

On 3 September 1939 war was declared, and that same day our little daughter Beth was born. While I was still in bed after her birth, the army took over the house as the second defence line ran through the park. 105 officers and 100 men moved into Melford Hall, and subsequently hundreds more men were billeted in Nissen huts in the park and grounds.

Willie, who was then 47 years old, was waiting to join his old regiment, in which as a young man he had served during the 1914–18 war. Meanwhile he joined the Home Guard but later that year he received very severe head injuries while on duty during the blackout. His injuries were so serious that he had to be sent to London, where Sir Harold Giles performed the operation and subsequent plastic surgery to save his face from being completely disfigured for life.

Sir Harold told me that when Willie left the King Edward VII hospital I would have to take him to a place of complete peace and quiet for at least a year if he was to recover fully—and even then he doubted if such a complete recovery was possible. But where? In East Anglia there was no peace. Where were we to go?

Suddenly Cousin Beatie came into my mind. I telephoned her. She said to me, 'Come here; bring him and the little ones.' (Richard was two years old and Beth had recently been born.) 'I will find somewhere for you to stay.' So off we went.

I had packed pram, cots, baby baths and baggage in a trailer behind a large hired car. Willie and I sat on the back seat with little Beth in a carry cot at our feet. Richard sat on Nanny's knee in front, and Mr Young, the owner of the car and the garage in Melford, drove us.

Willie was still ill and very weak and it took us two days to reach Sawrey.

I have hinted that Cousin Beatie did not express her feelings and emotions except in her art and writings and that she was not, therefore, demonstrative in any sense of that word. Yet when we entered Castle Cottage on our arrival, with me supporting Willie and holding on to little Richard as well, while Nanny followed behind carrying Beth, Cousin Beatie stared, startled, at us for a while in silence before these three words escaped from her: 'Oh, my dears!'—and in that short greeting the deep, deep feelings and the agony she felt at the sight of Willie and the rest of us was clearly expressed.

Cousin Willie had rushed forward and helped Willie into a chair. I took Beth from Nanny's arms and sat her on the Indian shawl on the dining-room table as I held on to her. Cousin Beatie looked and looked at her, and as she gazed her eyes shone as if tears were about to break through. She drew herself up to regain her usual composure and then uttered these words, words I have never forgotten: 'Now a baby is really sitting here on my table. Oh, something I did so long for.' And I realized that perhaps the dearest wish of her life had bypassed her. That she would have loved to have had children, I now knew.

In the days to come she would watch Richard and Beth, but in some strange way she kept at a distance in spite of her real interest and the enjoyment she derived from being in their presence. She kept two small dogs, to whom she was devoted, and she loved seeing the children laugh when she played with her dogs and made them do tricks. Yet one day she took a bar of chocolate (a rare and wonderful delicacy in wartime) from a drawer near her chair, and I clearly remember the glow of anticipation kindling in Richard's eyes. But Cousin Beatie broke the chocolate into small pieces and threw them one by one into the air for the dogs to catch. That a little boy of nearly three years old should long for a bit never occurred to her. Richard looked so disappointed and dejected when the last scrap of chocolate had been eaten by the dogs. There was no unkindness in her action: it was just that she liked watching the dogs doing their tricks and jumps and she took it for granted that everyone else would feel the same.

Cousin Beatie had found us rooms at the local inn; but Willie was so weak that the innkeeper's wife told me after a few days that she did not dare keep us. Again I turned to Cousin Beatie for help, and she replied, 'You know and understand what Hill Top means to me, therefore I shall let you all live there,' and she gave me the key. 'No one has slept there since I left,' she added.

I returned to Willie and the children with the problem solved. Nanny took care of the children while I went to the village shop to buy brooms, brushes, soap, pail and dusters to get Hill Top ready for our move. I surveyed the rooms, and decided that the children and Nanny had better sleep in the front rooms and Willie and I in the large square room at the back. The walls there were hung with great canvases of forest scenes painted by Cousin Beatie's brother and beside the bed stood a lovely old spinet. Wherever I opened drawers and chests they were packed with wonderful things. One drawer had the most lovely old dolls in it (I have always loved dolls, especially old ones, so I had a good look). A chest contained bonnets. How pretty they were with their various broad ribbons and other adornments. The chest stood in a sort of loft that you entered at first-floor level. Later, Cousin Beatie made me put on these various bonnets during one of her many visits to us. She so enjoyed seeing them displayed on a person.

Over the front porch and leading from the upstairs landing was a very small room which was used as a kind of box room, for it was full of all sorts of bits and pieces of furniture, boxes filled with oddments, and old household items. Among these things stood a small desk—not as grand as a davenport but superior to a school desk. Inside this, when lifting the top, I saw pages and pages written in the strangest and quite incomprehensible script. I wondered what on earth it could be. Now I think it must have been the diary she wrote in code.

Soon we were all installed at Hill Top farm. I do hope Cousin Beatie realized how grateful I was. Willie improved greatly there. He and Cousin Willie spent much time together, mostly fishing when Cousin Willie was free to do so. The children, the house and the cooking kept Nanny and me very busy, especially as the house, naturally, did not have the same conveniences as Melford. Coal was kept in the old pigsty, and we collected kindling and wood in the little spinney nearby. We used an oil stove for cooking. The peace and simplicity of lovely Hill Top farm did us all a great deal of good. The horrors of war and of the Gestapo in occupied countries, like my native Denmark, seemed further off.

Snapshots of the Hyde Parker family and Nanny at Hill Top. The photograph at the top, left, was taken by Beatrix Potter

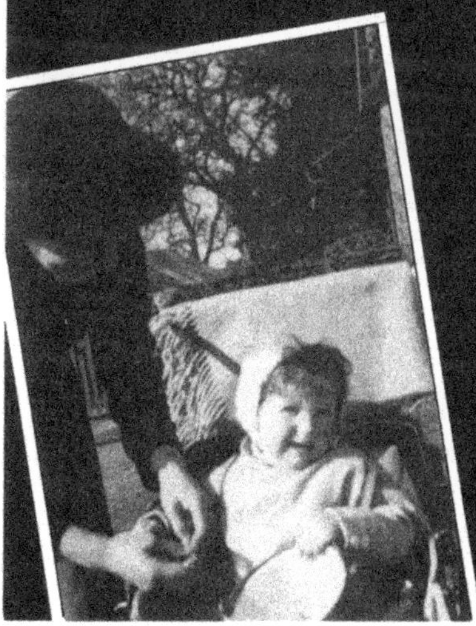

We visited Cousin Beatie often during the many months that followed, and she us. As I have mentioned, she enjoyed watching the children rather than talking to them. She who understood so well how to stir a child's imagination seemed rather shy of them. She knew a child from within, but how to catch their interest eluded her, and she realized this and stayed somewhat silent in their presence. Not only had she no children of her own; she told me that when she was a child she was not allowed to meet or mix with other children. 'My mother was so afraid we would catch germs,' she added.

I had met her mother, for during one of my early visits Cousin Beatie and I had driven across to Lake Windermere, where up a drive stood a stately house in which lived old Mrs Potter. All I can remember is a little old lady dressed in black, with black lace mittens, sitting in an armchair by the window, crocheting. I have never seen crocheting done so finely, with a hook as slim as a sewing needle and cotton as fine as sewing thread. It seemed incredible to me that any one, especially a very old lady, could see to do such fine work. This is all I remember of Mrs Potter, but I do remember Cousin Beatie saying, as we drove back, 'My mother does not approve of me living in a simple farm house. This she doesn't like at all.'

Christmas came, and with it deep snow. The lakes and tarns were covered with ice. This winter landscape was of an unearthly beauty. From a clear blue or rosy sky the sun shone on every hill, bush and tree, so everything glittered, down to the tiniest leaf and stone. I decided that all this called for a proper old-world Christmas, with a Christmas tree hung with glowing balls, sparkling tinsel and real candles which would cast their golden light all round the old kitchen at Hill Top. So a fine tree was cut and all the glorious decorations for it bought—and of course Cousin Beatie and Cousin Willie were invited.

Cousin Beatie, especially, was delighted with the thought that a real Christmas party was to be held at Hill Top. She brought a little soft toy, a marmalade cat, and mice to be put on the tree. 'The marmalade cat is for little Beth,' she said. And since the cat was in a lying down position it was easy to place it on one of the wide branches where it looked most comfortable and at home. For Richard she brought a blue elephant made of checked gingham, and a colourful wooden toy caravan complete with horse.

Christmas Day arrived, and when I saw Cousin Beatie

The marmalade cat given to Elizabeth Hyde Parker by Beatrix Potter

and Cousin Willie coming through the little gate and walking up the narrow path leading to the front door, I quickly lit the candles, so that the Christmas tree could be seen in all its glory as soon as they entered. But alas, alas! As soon as Cousin Beatie saw the tree with all its little flames, great fear and anxiety seized her. 'Put the candles out!' she called. And in great alarm, 'Put them out at once; the house will catch fire. Quickly, quickly put them out.'

We all obeyed. The children looked distressed, for how shortly, how terribly shortly, the beautiful and magic sight had lasted. Still, we soon comforted ourselves round the tea-table by the great, sweet-smelling log fire which not only gave out a delicious heat, but its great flames lit up the whole kitchen, and even the Christmas tree glowed in its soft light.

There was hot tea, a real iced Christmas cake (in spite of wartime), and many sweetmeats, nuts and rosy apples. So Cousin Beatie did, in the end, enjoy her Christmas party at Hill Top, despite her first shock and horror.

Once more I realized that Cousin Beatie's stern exterior and firm, almost forbidding manner hid many fears which she had carried within her since her childhood. Whatever she had heard, seen or assimilated from the grown-up world round her had left its mark on her sensitive nature. Now there was this fear of small flames in which she saw her whole house threatened by fire. It was like that fear of germs which might cause severe illness—her mother's great fear.

Cousin Beatie apparently had had the urge to write a 'proper book', as she called it. She spoke several times to me of her book *The Fairy Caravan*. 'I cannot understand

Beatrix Potter in the porch at Hill Top

The watercolour of mice, given to Ulla Hyde Parker by Beatrix Potter, was intended, perhaps, for 'The Solitary Mouse'

why that book has not become as much read and in as great demand as my shorter stories, which are after all mostly illustrations, and have not got much of the written word.' This fact disappointed her. She gave me a copy of that book and inside it she placed a beautiful watercolour of two little mice which she had painted. Then she picked up the white soft toy of Jemima Puddle-Duck, with its yellow felt legs and feet. She had dressed it up with the bonnet and Paisley shawl, so well-known from her book. 'I also want you to have this, for I used this model when I painted in the evenings. Yes, I would like you to have these things to remember me by.'

I was very touched and grateful. Yet could I ever forget Cousin Beatie? Could anyone forget her?

No. For Cousin Beatie belongs to those very few people who will always live within one.

The toy Jemima Puddle-Duck which Beatrix Potter used as a model for some of her book pictures

Ulla Hyde Parker was born in the university town of Copenhagen where she was educated. Her father was the Old Testament Scholar Christian Ditlef-Nielsen, and when she was old enough she was able to accompany him on some of his journeys abroad, especially to Oxford and Cambridge, which brought her in touch with the intellectual and artistic thoughts of the day.

It was on one of those visits to England that she met her future husband, Sir William Hyde Parker. Later she studied Art in Copenhagen, but this was interrupted by her marriage in 1931. After this, her life was fully occupied in taking care of her husband and children, and also Melford Hall, particularly at the end of World War II when Melford was in desperate need of restoration after extensive war damage and a fire in 1942.

She died in December 1998.

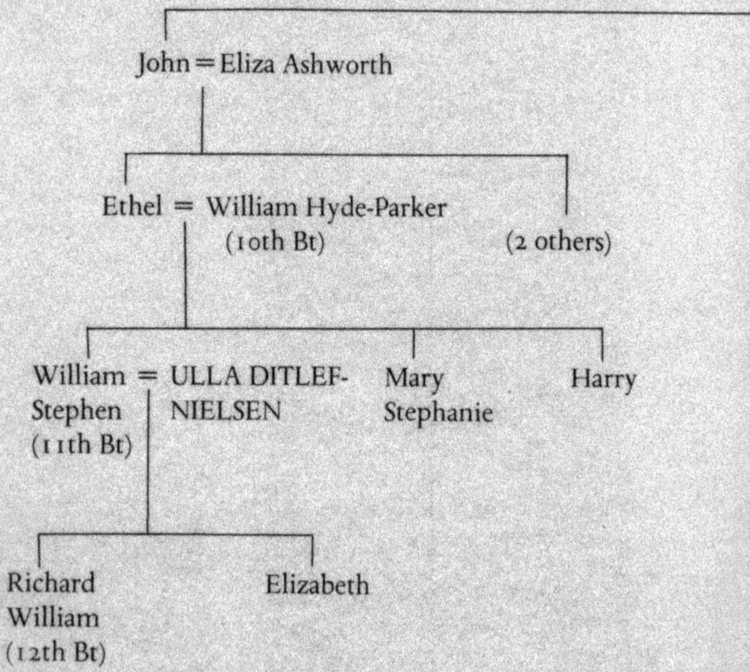
John = Eliza Ashworth
Ethel = William Hyde-Parker (10th Bt)
(2 others)
William Stephen (11th Bt) = ULLA DITLEF-NIELSEN
Mary Stephanie
Harry
Richard William (12th Bt)
Elizabeth

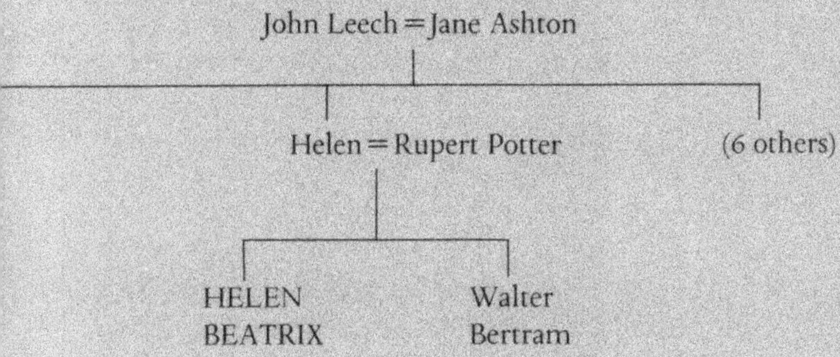


A Family Tree
showing the relationship
between
Beatrix Potter
and
Ulla Hyde Parker